DISNEY

YearBook
2007

FERN L. MAMBERG   Editorial Director
DEBBIE A. LOFASO   Creative Director
WALLY CHUNG   Production Manager

Stories and crafts illustrated by K. White Studio.

Stories on pages 14-25, 38-49, 60-71, 80-91, and all Disney character illustrations copyright © 2007 by Disney Enterprises, Inc.

Pages 14-25: Written by Catherine McCafferty. Pages 38-49: Written by Barbara Bazaldua. Pages 60-71: Written by Barbara Bazaldua. Pages 80-91: Written by Liane Onish. Pages 34-37: Art © Disney Enterprises, Inc. Based on the "Winnie the Pooh" works, by A.A. Milne and E.H. Shepard. All rights reserved. Pages 78-79: Art © Disney/Pixar.

Illustration Credits and Acknowledgments

6: © Cyril Ruoso/Minden Pictures. 7: © Gerald & Buff Corsi/Visuals Unlimited; © Frans Lanting/Minden Pictures; © Martin Harvey/DRK Photo. 8: © Art Wolfe/AllStock/PictureQuest. 9: © David Haring/OSF/Animals Animals; © Konrad Wothe/Minden Pictures. 10: © Scala/Art Resource, NY; The Granger Collection. 11: © Erich Lessing/Art Resource, NY; The Granger Collection. 12: ©Erich Lessing/Art Resource, NY; The Granger Collection. 13: ©Lilli Strauss/AP/Wide World Photos. 28: © Frans Lanting/Minden Pictures. 29: © Dr. Paul Zahl/Photo Researchers, Inc.; © Michael Fogden/DRK Photo. 30: © Jessie Cohen, The National Zoo/AP/Wide World Photos. 31: © Gregory K. Scott/Photo Researchers, Inc. 32: © Mark Moffett/Minden Pictures; © Gerald & Buff Corsi/Visuals Unlimited. 33: © Erwin & Peggy Bauer/Animals Animals. 34: © Edward Kinsman/Photo Researchers, Inc.; © Richard Hutchings/PhotoEdit. 35: © Ulf Battcher/Bilderberg/Peter Arnold, Inc.; © John Walker, *The Fresno Bee*/AP/Wide World Photos; poem by Edwina Fallis. 36: © Frieder Blickle/Bilderberg/Peter Arnold, Inc.; © Fred Newman, *The Evening News*/AP/Wide World Photos. 37: © John Warden/SuperStock; © Joe Gill, The Express-Times/AP/Wide World Photos. 50: © Frans Lanting/Minden Pictures. 51: © Tui De Roy/Minden Pictures; © 2003 Kim Keacox/DRK Photo. 52: © Patti Murray/Animals Animals; © Nancy Rotenberg/Animals Animals; © Phyllis Greenberg/Animals Animals; © Dennis M. David/Animals Animals. 53: © Tui De Roy/Minden Pictures; © Gerard Lacz/Animals Animals. 54: © Wayne Lynch/DRK Photo; © Tui De Roy/Minden Pictures. 55: © Heide Snell, Charles Darwin Foundation/AP/Wide World Photos. 56: © NASA-JPL. 57: © JHUAPL/SwRI; © John Raoux/AP/Wide World Photos; Mary Evans Picture Library. 58-59: © NASA/JPL; © Shigemi Numazawa/Atlas Photo Bank/Photo Researchers, Inc.; © NASA Goddard Space Flight Center. 74 © MPI/Getty Images; Hulton Archive/Getty Images. 75: © Library of Congress/AP/Wide World Photos. 76: © MPI/Getty Images. 77: © Nik Wheeler/Corbis; © Jeff Greenberg/PhotoEdit; © United States Mint image. 78: © Gerry Ellis/Minden Pictures; © Michael Habicht/Animals Animals. 79: © Stephen Dalton/Minden Pictures; © Schafer & Hill/Stone/Getty Images; © Tom Brakefield/Corbis; © Frans Lanting/Minden Pictures. 92: © Brian Bahr/Getty Images. 93: © Harry How/Getty Images; © Nancy Sheehan/PhotoEdit. 94: Hulton Archives/Getty Images. 95: © Jennifer Graylock/AP/Wide World Photos; © Robert Laberge/Getty Images.

Disney Year Book 2007

SCHOLASTIC INC.

New York • Toronto • London • Auckland • Sydney •
Mexico City • New Delhi • Hong Kong • Buenos Aires

Contents

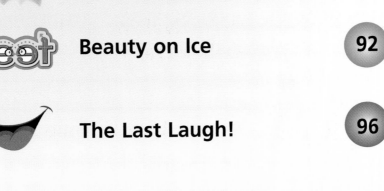

Wow! Your tail is really long!

The ringtail is the most common kind of lemur. Can you guess how the ringtail got its name?

LEAPIN' LEMURS!

Madagascar lies off the southeast coast of Africa. This beautiful island is home to animals that are found nowhere else in the world. Among them are the fascinating lemurs.

"Lemur" means "ghost of the night." Long ago, explorers in Madagascar's forests heard strange howls at night. They saw eyes glowing in the trees. They thought they were seeing ghosts! But they were seeing lemurs.

The 2-foot-long indri (left) is the biggest lemur. The 5-inch-long mouse lemur (above) is the smallest.

Lemurs are members of the primate family. That's the same animal family that monkeys, apes, and people belong to. But lemurs belong to a different branch of the family tree.

There are many kinds of lemurs. Some look like monkeys. Others look more like squirrels or mice. However, they all have some things in common.

Do you want to see how far I can leap?

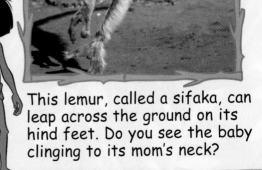

This lemur, called a sifaka, can leap across the ground on its hind feet. Do you see the baby clinging to its mom's neck?

Keeping an Eye on the Aye-Aye

The aye-aye is the strangest lemur of all. It's the size of a house cat. It has eyes like an owl, ears like a bat, and a nose like a rat. It has teeth like a beaver, so it can gnaw through tree bark. And it has a long bony middle finger that points in any direction! The aye-aye uses that finger to grab insects from under the tree bark.

The aye-aye is also the rarest lemur. Not many live in the wild. There are about 30 in captivity. Scientists hope to prevent these odd creatures from dying out.

Lemurs are gentle animals. They eat leaves, fruit, and insects. Some are busy during the day. Others sleep during the day and come out at night.

Lemurs have big eyes that help them see well in the dark. They can smell and hear very well, too. This helps them find food and stay safe from other animals that might want to eat a lemur.

Most lemurs spend nearly all their time in trees. They are great acrobats, leaping from branch to branch. Their hands have thumbs for grabbing branches and food. They use their long tails for balance.

Many lemurs live in family groups that are led by females. Baby lemurs use their hands to cling tightly to their mothers' fur. A baby may ride around on its mother's back for the first six months of its life.

Many kinds of lemurs love to eat berries (left). But the bamboo lemur (below) eats only bamboo. It spends all its time in bamboo groves, munching tender shoots.

Lemurs are my friends!

Lemurs are in danger of disappearing forever. People in many parts of Madagascar have cut down forests, leaving no place for lemurs to live. And they have hunted lemurs for food.

But now steps are being taken to save these wonderful animals and to protect their forest homes. The hope is that lemurs will always be leaping through the trees of Madagascar.

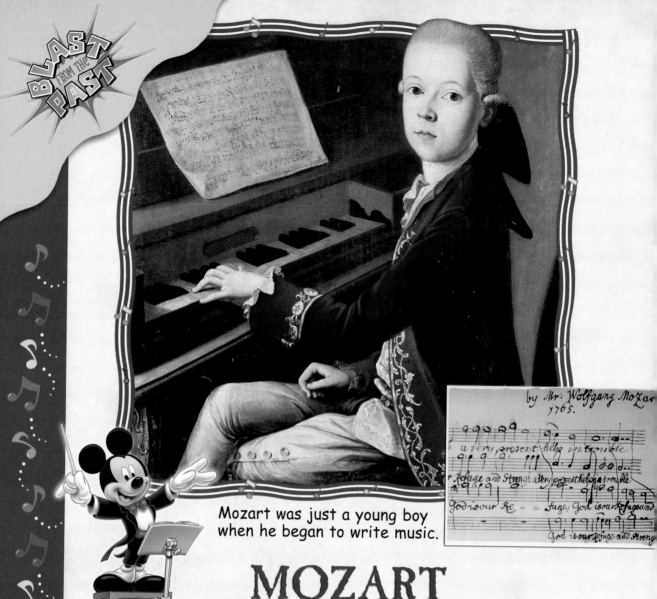

Mozart was just a young boy when he began to write music.

MOZART
A Musical Genius

He was playing music when he was 3 years old. He was writing music before he was 5. He grew up to become one of the greatest composers of all time. And his works are still played and loved today.

This musical genius was Wolfgang Amadeus Mozart. And 2006 was the 250th anniversary of his birth. All over the world, there were special events to celebrate his birthday.

The musical Mozarts: Leopold on the violin, Wolfgang at the keyboard, and Nannerl singing.

Mozart was born in 1756, in Salzburg, Austria. His father, Leopold, was a musician. The boy and his sister Nannerl both showed early talent for music. They were so amazing that Leopold had them perform for kings and queens in Europe. Wolfgang was just 6, and Nannerl was 11!

The Whiz Kid

Mozart was a "whiz kid"—a child prodigy. A child prodigy is a person who shows amazing talent at a young age. The talent may be in music or in any other field.

Little Wolfgang showed his talent at age 3. His father, Leopold, was teaching his sister Nannerl to play the harpsichord, an instrument like the piano. Wolfgang reached up to the keyboard and began to pick out notes.

Leopold began to teach his young son music, too. By the time Wolfgang was 4, he could play short pieces. At age 5 he was making up little dance tunes called minuets.

Child prodigies get lots of attention. When Wolfgang performed in public, he was called a "little magician"!

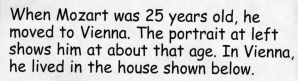

When Mozart was 25 years old, he moved to Vienna. The portrait at left shows him at about that age. In Vienna, he lived in the house shown below.

Mozart wrote his first symphony when he was just 8 years old. He wrote an opera when he was just 12! By age 15 he had a job. He wrote and played music for the Archbishop of Salzburg.

But Mozart was unhappy in Salzburg. The Archbishop treated him like a servant. After about ten years, he decided to leave. He went to live in Vienna, the capital of Austria.

To earn money, Mozart gave concerts. He taught music. And he sold his compositions. After a few years, he got a job writing music at the court of the Austrian Emperor.

Mozart also married in Vienna. He and his wife, Constanze, lived well. However, they were often short of money. To pay the bills, he worked as hard as he could.

To celebrate Mozart's birthday in 2006, kids and grown-ups in Vienna dressed up in clothes from his time. Then they danced a minuet!

Mozart was so busy writing music that he became tired and ill. But he kept working. Sadly, he died in 1791, at the age of 35.

Mozart died young. However, he left a great gift to the world—more than 800 pieces of beautiful music. He wrote symphonies, operas, and other great classical works. He also wrote cheerful tunes and funny songs. Many of his works are just as popular today as they were when he wrote them. Mozart's music will live on as long as there are people to listen to it.

Did You Know?

Some people think that listening to Mozart's music can give you a better memory. They call this "The Mozart Effect." Try it. Even if your memory doesn't improve, you'll enjoy the music!

Soon Enough

Bambi stepped up to the stream. He closed his eyes and bent his head.

Maybe today would be the day. He opened his eyes slowly and looked down into the water.

Still no antlers.

The water rippled, and Bambi's reflection quickly disappeared. "Whatcha doin', Bambi?" Thumper, his rabbit friend, poked a furry toe into the water.

"Just getting a drink." Bambi quickly began drinking.

"You look at yourself a lot when you get drinks," said Thumper.

"Well, I, uh. . ." Bambi didn't know what to say. He didn't want Thumper to know how much he wished for his antlers. He couldn't wait to have them. Every day, he looked for them. But every day, he was disappointed.

"Bambi just wants to make sure he won't be drinking up any frogs," said Bambi's friend Faline with a smile.

Bambi smiled back shyly. He had a feeling that Faline knew just what he was doing.

"Hey, who's hogging all the water?" Ronno, another young buck, shoved past Bambi. He splashed into the water, muddying it so that no one could get a clean drink.

"You'd better watch out for turtles," Flower the skunk told Ronno. "Bambi does."

"No, he was lookin' for frogs," corrected Thumper.

"Well, he should be looking for turtles," said Flower. "They're scarier!"

"I'm not scared of turtles or frogs. I'm not scared of anything!" Ronno puffed out his chest. "Anything gets in my way, I just give it a poke." Ronno tossed his head, showing off his growing antlers. "But I guess *you* can't do that, can you, Bambi?" He splashed closer to the bank where Bambi stood and peered at Bambi's head. "No antlers there! Just buds." Ronno gave a nasty laugh. "Maybe we should call you Buddy instead of Bambi."

16

"I'm not scared of turtles or frogs!" said Bambi. "And I don't need antlers to be brave!" Still, Bambi found himself backing away from Ronno.

"Well, come on and play-fight, then!" Ronno lowered his head. "Oh, never mind, I forgot. You need antlers to do that—Buddy."

"Let's go," Faline whispered to Bambi. "It's getting too crowded here," she added loudly, so Ronno would hear her.

"Yeah, go play with your little friends—Buddy!" Ronno called.

Bambi tried not to listen to Ronno's laughter, but it
seemed to echo through the trees. "Rabbits are lucky,"
Bambi said. "And skunks. And Faline, who's a doe.
None of you have to wait for antlers."

Thumper rolled on his back, laughing. "Me, with
antlers! Could you see that?"

Bambi turned away. "I think I want to be alone for a
while," he said.

"Oh, Bambi, you'll have your antlers soon enough,"
said Faline. "In the meantime, you've got friends who
like you just the way you are. I don't think Ronno will
ever have that."

"Thanks, Faline," said
Bambi. Her words did make
him feel better. Soon Bambi
was running and playing with
his friends. As he chased
Thumper through the woods,

Bambi saw a tangle of branches hanging down from a
tree. Carefully, he pulled the branches loose. The
branches settled around his ears and rose above his head.

Bambi stood very still. Then he shouted, "Look at me!
This is what I'll look like when I have antlers!" Bambi
ran back toward the
stream to look at himself.
Three steps later, his
branch-antlers fell off—
right at the feet of his
father, the Great Prince
of the Forest.

"H-hello, Father," said Bambi, trying to stand as straight and tall as he could.

"Hello, Great Prince," said his friends.

"Bambi, I think it's time we had a talk." The Great Prince stepped over the branches and led his son away. Bambi wondered if the Great Prince had seen him pretending to have antlers. His father's next words answered him.

"So, you think you're ready for antlers, son?" asked the Great Prince.

"Oh, yes, sir!" Bambi nodded. The Great Prince
stopped and looked down at him for a long moment.
"So," he said finally, "you think you're ready for all
the responsibilities that come to a growing buck?"

"Oh, yes!" said Bambi again.

"You're ready to help care for the herd? To fight off
enemies?"

Bambi thought about Ronno at the stream. He hadn't
even really wanted to play-fight with him.

"You're ready to leave behind your games with your friends?" his father continued.

Bambi thought some more. "If that's what having antlers means," he said slowly.

"That's what having antlers means, Bambi." His father nodded, then disappeared into the forest.

Bambi stood still. He had never thought about antlers that way. As he stood, he heard a loud rustling nearby.

Bambi peeked through the trees and saw a young buck struggling to free his antlers from a tangle of branches.

"Wait! I'll help you!" Bambi called. He ran over to the buck and pushed the branches loose.

"Thanks!" The buck shook his head in relief. "I'm still getting used to them." He rolled his eyes up toward his antlers. "They keep getting me stuck. Just wait," he said. "It'll happen to you soon enough!"

"Bambi!" Thumper popped out of a thicket. "Come on! We're going to play hide-and-seek with my sisters." He grinned. "I told them all to hide and not come out until we find them. We can take all afternoon if we want!"

Bambi turned to his new friend. "You can play, too."

The buck took one last look at the thicket. "No." He shook his antlers. "Those days are over for me."

Bambi watched as the buck carefully picked his
way through the forest. Then he raced after Thumper,
easily clearing the tangled branches of the thicket.
Bambi shook his head, feeling light and free.

He could wait for his antlers. They would come
soon enough.

Forest Fantasy

Collect materials from your forest friends' home—and bring nature into *your* home!

a pine branch

leaves

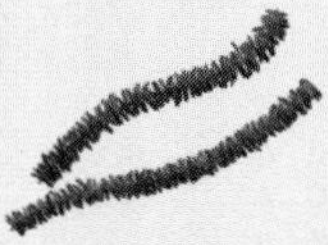

green pipe cleaners

white glue

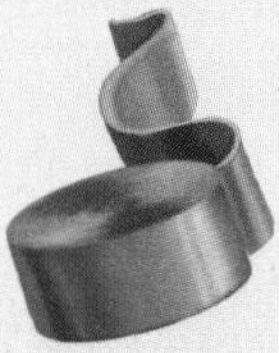

ribbon

acorns

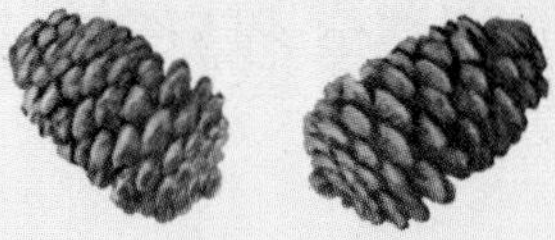

pinecones

wildflowers and berries

WHAT YOU DO

1. Use the green pipe cleaners to attach different kinds of leaves to the pine branch.

2. Carefully glue the pinecones to the branch.

3. Glue on the acorns, wildflowers, and berries.

4. Make a big, colorful bow. Tie it to the top of the pine branch.

Bambi and Thumper are sure to be pleased with your woodland decoration!

In many animal families, moms do all the work of raising babies. But in some animal families, the fathers help. And in a few cases, animal fathers go beyond the call of duty! Here are some of these special dads.

You are the King of Dads!

MR. MOM

Emperor penguins live in the Antarctic. It's cold and icy there. But these birds can keep their eggs and chicks warm.

When a female lays her egg, her mate takes over. He puts the egg on his feet and covers it with his belly. Mom heads for the ocean to catch and eat fish. Dad waits, keeping the egg warm.

In two months, the egg hatches. The dad keeps the new chick warm (above). He feeds it a milky liquid from his throat. At last the mom comes back. Now dad can leave and find food!

These two animal dads actually give birth to their babies. Amazing!

The male **seahorse** has a special pouch in his belly. The female puts her eggs right into his pouch. Then she swims away. Her job is done—but his is not. Inside the pouch, the eggs hatch into tiny seahorses. The babies grow for about six weeks. Then the male squeezes them out, one by one (top). There may be as many as 200!

A male **Darwin frog** scoops up a female's eggs with his mouth. The eggs drop into a special pouch that opens

from his throat. They hatch into tadpoles. The tadpoles grow and change into froglets. Then the male opens his mouth, and the little frogs hop out (above)!

This monkey is such a proud father!

Golden lion tamarins are beautiful monkeys that live in the rain forests of South America. In most monkey families, moms take care of the babies. But tamarins are different. The male golden lion tamarin is another special dad.

A female tamarin gives birth once a year. She nearly always has twins. The father takes each baby as soon as it is born. He carefully cleans its fur.

The babies cling tightly to him for the next six weeks (above). He keeps them safe as he scurries through the trees. He hands the babies to mom only at feeding time, so they can nurse. And when they begin to eat fruit and insects, he even chews their food to soften it!

Mother and father **woodpeckers** share the work of raising a family. These birds nest in holes in trees. They use their sharp beaks to chop out their tree-hole nests.

The female squeezes into the hole. She lays four to six eggs. Then the male and female take turns sitting on the eggs. After the chicks hatch, the parents take turns babysitting.

Sometimes the female stays in the nest with the chicks. The male hunts for insects to feed them. When he comes back, he drums on the tree with his bill. The female leaves, and he feeds the chicks (above). Now it's mom's turn to look for food.

Did You Know?

Baby woodpeckers grow up fast! After just four weeks, the youngsters are ready to fly. Their parents feed them for a few days longer, until they are ready to live on their own.

These two animal dads carry their babies piggyback!

A male **dart-poison frog** guards the female's eggs until they hatch. Then the tiny tadpoles wiggle onto his sticky back (right).

The tadpoles ride around on their dad for several weeks. Sometimes he jumps in a pool to keep them moist. They grow bigger. One day, when the male takes a dip, they jump off and swim away.

A **giant waterbug** is a super dad, too. The female lays her eggs right on his back (left)! She glues them on, so they won't fall off.

These bugs like to fly around at night. But with the eggs on his back, the male is too heavy to fly. He stays in his pond until the eggs hatch, and the young bugs go off on their own.

Hop on my back and go for a ride!

A **wolf** pack is like a big family. It's made up of the mom and dad and their pups. Often there are aunts and uncles, too.

Pups are born in the spring. At first they sleep in the den with their mom. The male sleeps outside to guard them. He and the other wolves go hunting. They bring back food for the pups.

As the pups grow, the father visits them. He sniffs them. He licks their fur. He may even let them crawl all over him! Before long, the pups are old enough to play outside the den with their father (above).

Season's

WINTER

Winter. . .spring. . .summer. . .fall. . . every year has four seasons. And each season is special in its very own way. Which time of year do you like the best?

Winter is the coldest season. The trees have no leaves. Their branches shake in the chilly wind. In the North, ice covers ponds and lakes. Snow falls. Tiny snowflakes look like bits of lace. They pile up, covering the ground with white. Kids put on warm coats, hats, and scarves to go outside.

What a great time to build a snowman!

Look! I can catch snowflakes on my tongue!

See the pretty snowflakes
Falling from the sky;
On the wall and housetops
Soft and thick they lie.

Greetings

SPRING

The sun is shining. The air is warm. The grass is green. After the long winter, spring is finally here!

In spring, nature wakes up from its long winter nap. Trees put out new green leaves. Flowers begin to bloom. They fill the air with their sweet scents. Bees come buzzing. Birds sing. And soft spring breezes blow. Everyone wants to play outside in spring. A breezy spring day is perfect for running, jumping, and flying a kite!

Spring makes me bounce!

Little Johnny Jump-up said,
"It must be spring,
I just saw a lady-bug
And heard a robin sing."

SUMMER

Summer days are long and warm. Gardens are filled with flowers. The sun rises early and sets late. There's plenty of time for fun! Schools are closed, and kids are on vacation. Some families take trips or go camping.

Summer is a great time for outdoor games and sports. You can ride a bike. You can play ball with your friends. But summer days are also great for just taking it easy. Sometimes it's just too hot to do anything but relax. On those hot days, lots of people cool off at the beach or at the swimming pool. And nothing tastes better on a hot day than cool, delicious ice cream! Yum!

I have a little garden,
And every summer day,
I dig it well,
I rake it well,
And pull the weeds away.

FALL

Nights are cool. The days are getting shorter. Fall is here. It's time to go back to school.

Many leaves change color in the fall. They turn bright orange, yellow, red, and brown. Then they let go of their branches. They tumble through the air to the ground. Piles of leaves make crunching sounds as you walk through them.

Halloween comes at the end of October. Kids carve pumpkins to make jack-o'-lanterns. They put on costumes and go "trick or treating"!

Did You Know?

Trees that lose their leaves in the fall are called deciduous trees. Trees that keep their leaves are called evergreens.

"Come," said the Wind to the Leaves one day.
"Come over the meadow and we will play.
Put on your dresses of red and gold.
For summer is gone and the days grow cold."

A FESTIVAL FOR OAKEY OAKS

Chicken Little and his friends were munching veggie burgers at the Feedbag Cafe when Turkey Lurkey, the mayor of Oakey Oaks, came in. He looked very sad.

"Excuse me, Mr. Mayor," Chicken Little said politely. "Is something wrong?"

"Yes," Turkey Lurkey replied. "All the pep and perkiness have gone from Oakey Oaks. After all the excitement in town, everyone's bored now. They feel like there's nothing fun to look forward to."

"That's terrible!" Chicken Little exclaimed. "There's always some way to have fun!"

"Well, Chicken Little," Turkey Lurkey replied, "if you can figure out a way to bring the pep back to Oakey Oaks, I'll personally give you a medal!" With a heavy sigh, he wandered out of the cafe.

Chicken Little and his friends looked at each other.

"We have to do something to perk up Oakey Oaks," Chicken Little said. "Think of something—fast!"

"We could say 'the earth is rising' instead of 'the sky is falling,'" Runt said.

"We could say we saw the Mock Mess Monster in the town swimming pool," suggested Abby.

Chicken Little shook his head. "No more disasters— please!" he begged. Suddenly he had an idea.

"The Aliens loved our acorns," he said. "Let's have an Intergalactic Acorn Festival. Oakey Oaks will be famous throughout the galaxy!"

"That's a terrific idea," Abby cheered. "We'll get the whole town involved. Let's do it!"

Soon all the folks in Oakey Oaks were happily doing their best for the Acorn Festival. Chicken Little put up posters. Runt made sign-up sheets for people to bring homemade acorn treats. Fish planned games and contests. Abby designed an acorn cap and T-shirt for everyone to wear.

Townspeople bustled about all day, picking acorns by the wheelbarrow. The Farmer in the Dell offered his field for the festival grounds. Soon the air rang with the sounds of hammers and saws. In the center of the festival grounds, Abby glued thousands of acorns together to create a statue of an Alien munching acorns.

At last the day of the festival arrived. Orange and brown banners flapped in the breeze, and the scent of roasted, salted acorns filled the air. As the school band began to play, the people of Oakey Oaks poured into the festival grounds wearing their acorn hats and T-shirts. They joked and laughed as they carried in bags, baskets, buckets, and barrels of acorn treats to share.

When everything was ready, they waited for the Aliens. They waited. And waited. But no one came.

At last, as the sun set, the band stopped playing.
The laughter and chatter died down. Silence fell over
the festival grounds. Slowly, the townspeople began
to leave.

"This was just another of your lame-cluck ideas,
Chicken Little," they muttered. "When are we ever
going to learn not to listen to you!"

Finally only Chicken Little and his friends were left in the empty festival grounds.

"I guess it *was* a dumb idea," Chicken Little said.

"It was not!" Abby insisted. "Those Aliens don't know what they missed!" Then she gasped. "Oh my! They really don't know what they missed—we forgot to tell them! They didn't come because they didn't know!"

"But Abby," Runt protested, "the Aliens are miles above the earth. How could we tell them about the festival?"

"We need a big lighted sign!" Abby and Chicken Little both exclaimed. "Lights! We need lots and lots of lights. Come on!"

Chicken Little and his friends raced into town. In a short while they were back at the festival grounds, trailing miles of Christmas tree lights. Quickly they draped the lights across the field to make a huge sign that read: "First Intergalactic Acorn Festival Tonight! Land Here!" Then they plugged in the cords. The festival grounds lit up with thousands of lightbulbs.

"Wowser!" Abby sighed. "It's beautiful!"

"Uh-oh," Runt said. "Look at Oakey Oaks."

The friends whirled around in time to see all the lights in Oakey Oaks blink out. Their sign had drained all the electricity from the town. It was now pitch-black.

"I'm gonna hear about this," Chicken Little sighed. Sure enough, within minutes townspeople began to rush toward the fairgrounds, flashing their car lights and waving candles and flashlights.

"Chicken Little, what have you done this time?" the mayor shouted.

But as the angry townspeople stormed toward Chicken Little, a humming sound filled the air. Colored lights flashed above them. And suddenly an Alien spaceship landed, followed by another and another.

The townspeople stared as hundreds of Aliens in every shape, size, and color poured from the ships and raced toward the festival, making happy, excited noises.

Quickly the school band began to play. Soon, Aliens and townspeople were dancing together. They joined in games of acorn toss and entered the  pie-eating contest. They munched treats and ran races. Everyone was having a wonderful time!

At last, the festival was over. As the spaceships lifted off, the Oakey Oakians waved good-bye. "Same time next year!" they shouted, and the spaceships blinked their lights in reply.

Turkey Lurkey marched up to Chicken Little and his friends and pinned big blue ribbons on them. "I hereby declare Chicken Little and his friends the Official Founders of the Oakey Oaks Intergalactic Acorn Festival," he announced to cheers and applause.

Chicken Little was very proud of his blue ribbon, but what made him happiest were the smiling faces he saw. He and his friends had given the townspeople something to look forward to every year, and that was the best reward of all.

A giant tortoise gazes over the slopes of the Galápagos Islands. Doesn't it look like a creature from another age?

Islands Lost in Time

Where can you see animals like no others in the world? In the amazing Galápagos Islands!

The Galápagos Islands are in the Pacific Ocean. They lie off the coast of the South American country of Ecuador.

The British scientist Charles Darwin made these islands famous. Darwin visited the islands in 1835. He saw plants and animals found nowhere else.

Did You Know?

Spanish sailors named the Galápagos Islands. "Galápagos" means "tortoises" in Spanish. Giant tortoises are among the islands' most famous animals.

Darwin figured out that the plants and animals came to the islands long, long ago. But the islands were very far out at sea. So the plants and animals that reached the islands were cut off from others of their kind.

Over the ages, they slowly became different from their mainland cousins. They developed in ways that helped them live in their new island home. Today, most Galápagos animals are found only on these islands!

A Sally Lightfoot crab scampers across a rock. There are many of these crabs in the Galápagos.

Hi there, odd-looking creature!

Galápagos marine iguanas are the world's only seagoing lizards. They can stay underwater for 30 minutes!

Galápagos Plants

Plants came to the Galápagos Islands before animals. Winds and ocean currents carried seeds from the mainland. Passing birds may have dropped seeds, too.

Only some of the seeds could sprout and grow. The islands are rocky, hot, and dry. The plants had to be tough to survive. Many of these plants aren't found anywhere else.

In the driest parts of the islands, cacti thrive. Some, like the prickly-pear cactus, grow quite big. These desert plants store water in their stems. They don't need much rain.

Some parts of the islands get more moisture. There, grasses and small trees grow. So do flowering vines, such as passionflowers, poincianas, and Jerusalem thorns.

passionflower

Jerusalem thorn

poinciana

prickly-pear cactus

I'm glad I can fly!

A cormorant is a seabird that dives to catch fish. Cormorants are found in many places. But the cormorants of the Galápagos (above) are different from all others. They can't fly!

The ancestors of these birds probably

A Galápagos sea lion mom cuddles her pup.

came from South America. In the Galápagos, they found lots of fish. And there were no predators—animals that hunt other animals. Thus the cormorants didn't need to fly. Eventually, their wings became useless.

Galápagos sea lions are also special. They are super swimmers. And like many animals on the islands, they aren't afraid of people. Sea lion pups will even jump into boats!

53

How does a male frigate bird catch a female's eye? He puffs out a big red heart-shaped pouch on his chest!

Many kinds of seabirds visit the Galápagos Islands each year. They come to find mates, to nest, and to raise their young. One of the most colorful visitors is the frigate bird. Other island visitors include comical-looking birds called boobies.

I can dance better than you!

Male and female blue-footed boobies dance! The male starts the dance. He points his bill up, whistles, and rocks from side to side.

Galápagos tortoises are true giants. They can weigh 600 pounds! And they can live to be 150 years old. They lumber across the land, eating plants.

In Darwin's time, there were about 250,000 Galápagos tortoises. But their numbers have dropped sharply since then. In the past, sailors stopped at the islands to hunt the tortoises for meat. Hunting nearly wiped them out. And people brought goats and other animals to the islands. The goats ate the plants that the tortoises needed to survive.

There are only about 15,000 tortoises today. But now people are working to protect them. They want the tortoises and all the other wonderful animals of the Galápagos to survive.

Lonesome George

Different kinds of Galápagos tortoises live on different islands. And a tortoise that's been nicknamed Lonesome George is the last of his kind.

Lonesome George was found years ago on Pinta Island. He was the only tortoise there. Today he lives at a research station on Santa Cruz Island. Scientists there breed Galápagos tortoises and then return them to their home islands. This will increase the number of tortoises.

The scientists hoped that George, now 70 years old, would mate with a female from another island. So far, he hasn't met the right match!

Pluto: Out of the Planet Club

Pluto (left) and its moon Charon (above) are far, far away. In this picture, added color makes them seem to glow. But they are really dim and very hard to see, even with a big telescope.

How many planets travel around our sun? Until 2006, the answer was nine. But now the answer is eight! Scientists say that one of the nine, Pluto, isn't really a planet at all.

Pluto is far out at the edge of the solar system. It doesn't get much of the sun's warmth and light. It's a cold, dark world. And it's very small. It's just not the same as the eight major planets, scientists say.

Planet or not, scientists want to learn more about Pluto. In 2006 the U.S. National Aeronautics and Space Administration (NASA) sent an unmanned spacecraft speeding toward it.

The spacecraft is called *New Horizons*. It will be the first ever to visit Pluto. But that icy world is so far away, it will take the spacecraft nine years to get there!

Hey! I'm called Pluto, too!

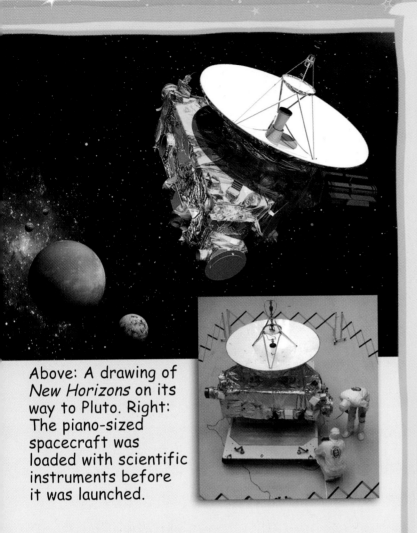

Above: A drawing of *New Horizons* on its way to Pluto. Right: The piano-sized spacecraft was loaded with scientific instruments before it was launched.

When *New Horizons* reaches Pluto, it will scan the icy surface. It will check the thin blanket of gases, or atmosphere, around Pluto. And it will send pictures back to scientists on Earth.

New Horizons will also check out Pluto's moon Charon. Charon is a strange moon. It's almost half as big as Pluto!

Naming Pluto

Pluto is named for the Roman god of the underworld (below). This name was the idea of an 11-year-old British girl, Venetia Burney.

In 1930, Venetia's grandfather read about the discovery of what was thought to be a new planet. He asked Venetia what she thought it should be called.

Venetia knew that other planets were named for Greek and Roman gods. She said that Pluto would be a good name for this dark, faraway world. Her grandfather passed her idea along. And the name Pluto was chosen over dozens of others.

A Dwarf Planet

This picture shows Pluto's place in the solar system. For many years, everyone thought this faraway world was the ninth planet.

Now Pluto has been voted out of the planet club. Why? Scientists are using new, powerful telescopes to look into space. They have found more objects like Pluto on the edge of the solar system. At least one of these objects is bigger than Pluto!

Could all these objects be planets? Or should they—and Pluto—be called something else? In August 2006, scientists from around the world met to answer that question. They decided that Pluto and objects like Pluto aren't true planets. They are now called "dwarf planets."

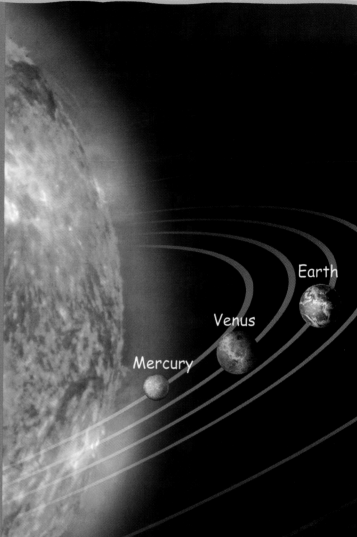

Earth

Venus

Mercury

Pluto itself is strange. It's round, like Earth and the other planets. But it isn't a rocky ball, like Earth. And it's not a giant gas ball, like Jupiter. Instead, it's made of ice and rock. And it's tiny. It's less than half the size of the smallest planet, Mercury.

Small is beautiful!

Did You Know?

Our home planet, Earth, is more than five times bigger than Pluto. Five Plutos could easily fit inside Earth!

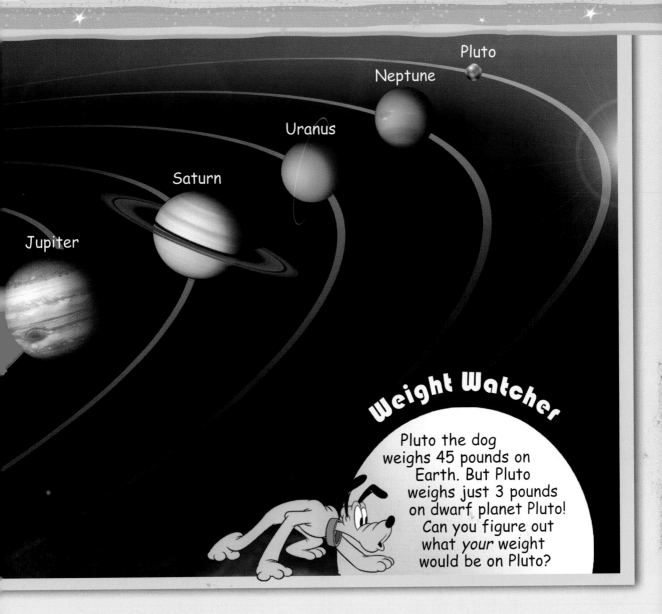

Weight Watcher

Pluto the dog weighs 45 pounds on Earth. But Pluto weighs just 3 pounds on dwarf planet Pluto! Can you figure out what *your* weight would be on Pluto?

Because Pluto is so small, its gravity is weak. Gravity is the force that keeps your feet on the ground. It gives objects weight. On Pluto, you would weigh far less than you do on Earth.

So far, scientists have only blurry pictures of Pluto. They hope *New Horizons* will be able to solve some of its mysteries. Then, after leaving Pluto, the spacecraft will travel on. Out beyond Pluto, other icy objects travel around the sun. What will *New Horizons* find?

If The Shoe Fits!

"Your room is a mess!" King Triton said as he stood at the door of the bedroom that Ariel shared with her sisters. "We have guests from across the seven seas coming to the palace tonight for the Sea Foam Ball. I want this room sparkling clean, or none of you are going!"

"That's not fair!" Alana said. She was sitting next to Aquata at her dressing table, trying on a new hair ornament. The table was covered with jars of powder, polish, and perfume.

Ariel's sisters turned away from their sea-lace scarves and jeweled tops. "We can't miss the ball!" Aquata exclaimed. "We've been getting ready for days!"

"We have appointments to get our fins polished," Alana added. "We can't clean our room now! Besides, a lot of this is Ariel's mess."

Ariel's bed was heaped with shells and pebbles. Between the pillows lay a baby octopus named Squirt, who had a sore tentacle that Ariel was nursing.

"I don't care whose mess this is!" King Triton thundered. "Get it cleaned up—or no ball for any of you girls!"

The sisters turned to Ariel, smiling sweetly at her.

"Please, Ariel," they begged. "Will you clean the room? We don't have time to do it and get ready for the ball. We have to leave for our fin-polishing appointment."

Reluctantly, Ariel agreed. She thought balls were dumb, but she knew how much her sisters loved balls and wanted to go.

Alana stopped at the door. "Be extra careful with my new hair ornament," she said. "It's very delicate!"

As Ariel looked around the messy room, Flounder swam in. "Whatcha doin'?" he asked.

"My sisters talked me into cleaning our room," Ariel said. "I said I would, but it's so messy. It'll take hours!"

"I know a fast way to clean," said Flounder. "Go get some kelp trash nets from the kitchen."

When Ariel
returned with the
kelp trash nets,
Flounder swished
his tail and swept
everything off Alana's
dressing table into one
of the nets.

"See? Just shove everything in the nets, then put them behind the seaweed. And the room is clean!"

Ariel and Flounder danced around the room. *Swoosh!* Into the bags went clothes and scarves and jewelry. *Swish!* In went Ariel's shells and pebbles. But all the swishing and swooshing startled Squirt. With a squeak, the little octopus squiggled off the bed and darted around, squirting ink everywhere.

"Come here, Squirt! Come here!" Ariel called, chasing Squirt around the room. But Squirt's ink made it hard to see. Ariel tripped over a net, lost her balance, and sat down hard on it. There was a loud crunch!

"Uh-oh," Ariel said as she pulled Alana's new hair ornament from the net. She hadn't meant to break the ornament. What would Alana wear to the ball now?

Ariel turned to Flounder. "What am I going to do?"

"You're good at making pretty things," Flounder replied. "Just make Alana another hair ornament."

"Terrific idea!" Ariel exclaimed. "But I need something really special to make it with!"

Ariel grabbed
her collecting bag.
"Come on, Flounder!
The room's clean.
Let's go!"

Together, Flounder and Ariel looked and looked all
over the ocean. They found shells, pearls, and sea
flowers, but they didn't find anything extra-special.

Just then, a shadow passed above them and they heard
voices—human voices—laughing!

"Ohmigosh!" Flounder cried. "We were so busy looking
for treasures, we almost swam to the surface! We have
to go back down right now!"

"Let's take a peek first," Ariel said. She knew she was forbidden to go to the surface, but she felt so curious about the laughing human voices.

At last, Flounder agreed. Slowly, carefully, Ariel and Flounder peeked the tiniest peek above the waves.

Before them was a pretty little boat. A human boy and girl sat in it, laughing and talking. As Ariel and Flounder watched, the girl stood up and tried to move to the other side of the boat. It rocked and tilted dangerously.

"Sit down, or you'll fall in!" the boy human shouted.

"I just want to get my parasol," the girl replied. Just then, a large wave smacked the boat. The girl lost her balance, and with a startled cry, she fell into the sea.

The boy dove into the water after her. But Ariel was faster. She swam after the girl, caught her sash, and pulled her to the surface. Flounder and Ariel heaved and shoved the girl back into the boat. They dove from sight just as the boy surfaced, gasping for breath. Luckily, neither human had seen Ariel and Flounder.

But Ariel was very upset. She had dropped her collecting bag while helping the girl who had fallen out of her boat. And now she had *nothing* to make Alana's hair ornament! She swam back and forth, until she finally found her bag. Right next to it she saw something gleaming, and she quickly picked it up. It was pink with sparkly jewels and long flowing ribbons. The middle was hollow, like a shell.

"What is it?" Flounder asked.

"I really don't know what it's called," Ariel answered. "But once I saw two of them on a woman's whatchamacallems— her feet! It's just what I need for Alana."

"But, Ariel," said Flounder, "Alana doesn't have feet! What is she going to do? Wear it on her head?"

"Sort of!" she answered. "Come on! I have work to do!"

The moment she returned home, Ariel took the jewels and ribbons off the pink object. She then glued and stitched and turned them into something quite different. She finished just as her sisters swam into the room. They were delighted to see how neat it was.

Then Alana noticed her dressing table. "Where's my hair ornament?" she asked.

"I accidentally broke it," Ariel explained. "I didn't mean to. I'm sorry."

"No!" Alana wailed. "What can I put in my hair now? What can I possibly wear to the ball tonight?"

"You could wear this," Ariel answered, handing Alana the new hair ornament. "I made it for you!"

The little hair
ornament gleamed
with jewels and a
bouquet of shells. Sea flowers
and tiny pearls were glued to the pretty
pink ribbons that trailed from it.

"It's beautiful!" Alana gasped as she tied
it onto her head and gazed in the mirror.

That night, Alana's hair ornament was the talk of all
the mermaids at the ball. Ariel dreamily watched
Alana dancing with Prince Waverly—and she thought
of all the wonderful human treasures just waiting for
her to find under the sea!

Under-the-Sea Pasta Creatures

Sebastian says that under the sea is the best place to be! Using dry pasta and paint, create your own under-the-sea place to be.

What You Need

blue construction paper

different kinds of dry pasta

grains of rice

white glue

colored markers

food coloring

google eyes

What You Do

1. Decide what you want your pasta creatures to look like. Color the pasta shapes with the markers or the food coloring.

2. Glue the grains of rice onto the blue paper. This will be sand at the bottom of the ocean.

3. Glue your pasta creatures along the top of the rice grains. Add other pasta pieces to create seaweed and coral.

4. Add google eyes to your creatures.

Ariel and Sebastian will be right at home in your seascape!

This painting shows Jamestown, Virginia, a few years after it was founded.

THE JAMESTOWN COLONY

In the spring of 1607, three ships reached the coast of what is now Virginia. They had sailed across the Atlantic Ocean from England. The people on board the ships had come to settle in a new land. They were the founders of Jamestown, England's first lasting colony in North America.

Jamestown turns 400 years old in May 2007. And Americans are celebrating the birthday. From that small start in Jamestown, the United States was born.

The English settlers arrive at Jamestown. They begin to cut trees to build a fort.

74

The first settlers were a group of 104 men and boys. They called their settlement Jamestown in honor of King James I of England. They built it on a river, which they named the James River. The settlers weren't the first people in this land. American Indians already lived there.

The settlers mostly wanted to search for gold. They weren't interested in farming. Soon their food ran out. People began to get sick. Jamestown almost didn't make it.

Only about 40 people lived through the first winter. They all might have died. But then Captain John Smith took charge.

Pocahontas, you are a brave woman!

POCAHONTAS: THE COLONISTS' FRIEND

Soon after reaching Virginia, Captain John Smith was captured by Indians. A story says that Pocahontas, the daughter of Chief Powhatan, saved his life. The chief ordered Smith killed. But Pocahontas begged her father to let him live (right). And the chief did.

No one knows if the story is really true. But Pocahontas was a good friend to the colonists. She later married the Englishman John Rolfe.

Smith asked the Indians to give food to the starving settlers. And he made the settlers stop looking for gold. Instead, they learned to fish, hunt, and grow crops for food. Ships came from England with supplies. More settlers came, too.

But the settlers weren't very good at farming. The harvests were poor. The colony was barely getting by. Then, in 1609, Smith was wounded. He had to go back to England. That winter, hunger and sickness hit Jamestown again.

JAMESTOWN FESTIVAL PARK

Jamestown was set on a swampy spit of land on the James River. It was damp, and the land wasn't good for farming. Over the years, people left it for better places in Virginia. The original Jamestown is now gone. But you can see what it was like at Jamestown Festival Park.

The settlers trade with the Indians at Jamestown. Without the help of the Indians, the colony might not have lasted.

The park is near the site of the original settlement. It has copies of the fort and houses that the first settlers built. There are also full-scale models of the three ships that brought the first settlers from England.

Actors in Colonial costumes play the parts of settlers, sailors, and other people you might have met in Jamestown 400 years ago. They show how life was lived way back then.

The colonists almost gave up. But new supplies and settlers arrived at the last minute. Slowly, the colony began to thrive.

In time, 12 more English colonies were founded. In 1776 these colonies declared their independence. They became a new nation— the United States of America!

DID YOU KNOW?

Virginia's new state quarter celebrates the founding of Jamestown. It shows the three ships that brought the first settlers.

And the Winner Is...

What contests could these odd-looking animals win? The South American king vulture (top) gets the lumpy-nose award. And the star-nosed mole (bottom) gets the prize for the weirdest nose. Check out those "nose rays"!

I win the scariest blue-monster prize!

I win the biggest-eye award!

The axolotl (above), a kind of salamander with feathery gills, wins the space-alien look-alike contest. The hoatzin (right) wins the wildest-hair prize. The male mandrill (bottom, left), a baboon, wins the most-colorful-face award. And the male elephant seal (bottom, right) wins first prize for nose size—and its nose is still growing!

A Wild Ride for Princess Minnie

Princess Minnie was much loved in her princess-dom. She personally paid all the merchants with gold coins from her gold mines. Today, she paid the butcher, the baker, and the candlestick maker. Then she paid the tinker and the tailor. But when it came to Sir Goofy and Sir Mickey, she found that she had run out of gold!

The princess called for another chest of gold coins, but there were no more gold-filled chests. There was no more gold in her mines, either. Her princess-dom was broke!

"Oh, dear!" exclaimed Princess Minnie. "What will we do?" She turned to her knights. "I am so sorry, Sir Mickey and Sir Goofy. There is no more gold to pay you."

"Gawrsh, your Princess-ness, that's okay," said Sir Goofy. "We can come back tomorrow." He bowed, then tripped over his own two knightly feet.

"It is I who am sorry, Sir Goofy. My princess-dom is broke. I have no gold to pay my brave knights. I have no gold to take care of my people!" she said with a sob.

Sir Mickey, whose favorite princess and person in the whole wide world was Minnie, said, "Don't worry, Your Highness. We will find a new gold mine!"

Sir Goofy said, "We will? Gawrsh, sure we will!"

"We will not return empty-handed!" Sir Mickey promised.

"What do you know about gold mining, Goofy?" Mickey asked, as they drove away from the palace on their horse-drawn wagon.

"Gee, Mickey, I guess I know as much as you do." This was really too bad. In knight school, Mickey and Goofy had learned to ride and fight with swords, to save damsels in

distress, and to climb tall trees to rescue frightened kittens—although, as Sir Goofy recalled, he hadn't done too well in the kitten-rescue course.

"We've been rewarded for many good deeds," Mickey pointed out, "but never for finding a gold mine."

The two knights traveled miles and miles without seeing a single mine. All they saw was a sad giant troll.

"Good day, giant
troll. We are Sir Mickey
and Sir Goofy. You look so sad. Can we do anything to
save you from your sadness?" Sir Mickey asked.

Sighing a sad giant troll sigh, the troll said, "Oh. No.
There's nothing two knights can do to save me. I'm
Sad Sid, the lonely giant troll."

"Gosh, Sad Sid, why are you so lonely?" Sir Mickey
asked.

Sad Sid pointed to the mountain behind him. "Ever
since my mine ran out of gold many years ago, no one
comes by to visit, not even to watch me juggle." Sad
Sid removed three large sparkly rocks from his troll
knapsack and began to perform. Then he asked, "Do
knights juggle?"

Sir Goofy said, "Nope. No juggling. Just riding and sword-fighting, saving damsels in distress, and climbing trees to rescue kittens—like that little gray one over there!" And off Sir Goofy ran to demonstrate.

Uh-oh! Sir Goofy reached for the kitten, but he only frightened it. The kitten leaped onto the knights' horse, spooking it. As the horse ran to get away, it wedged itself and the wagon between a tree and a giant boulder.

"Hmmm," said Sad Sid, putting his sparkly juggling rocks back into his troll knapsack. "It looks like it's you knights who need saving!"

The troll and the knights tried to push the boulder out of the way. "Okay, boys," said Sir Mickey, "One, two, three, push!" They pushed. They heaved. They shoved. The boulder wouldn't budge.

"Gawrsh, Mickey, now what will we do?" asked Sir Goofy. They all climbed into the wagon to think. Sad Sid stretched his long legs and rested his feet on the tree. The troll pushed against the tree. The boulder budged just a bit. "That's it!" said Sir Mickey. The knights shoved and the troll pushed. The boulder budged a bit more and began to rock, and then it finally rolled down the hill.

But as
soon as
the boulder
started to roll,
it released a huge
burst of water from
a hidden spring. The
wagon rose up on the
powerful geyser of water.

"Whoa! Wow! Wheee!"
cried Sad Sid, Sir Mickey,
and Sir Goofy, as they slid
down the flow of rushing
water and made a splash
landing—right in Princess
Minnie's moat! Princess
Minnie couldn't believe
her eyes!

"Garwsh! That
was some ride!"
said Sir Goofy,
shaking the
water off his
armor.

"That was the most fun I've had since there was gold in my mine!" said Sad Sid.

"Princess Minnie!" cried Sir Mickey. "We huffed and puffed and pushed and shoved and finally moved a giant, huge, really, really big boulder! Then water gushed up and carried us all the way back to the palace! What a wild water ride! Gosh, it would be so great to do it again! I bet even Your Highness would love a really wild water ride!"

"Everybody would!" added Sir Goofy.

Princess Minnie smiled and said, "Yes, I'm sure I would. But, please, who is this really, really big person?"

"Sorry, Your Highness," said Sir Mickey. "Please meet Sad Sid, the lonely giant troll."

Sid may have been a lonely giant troll, but he did have manners. Bowing to the princess, Sid held out his troll knapsack. "Princess," he said, "my mine ran out of gold long ago, so I have no gold to give you as a sign of my respect. But please accept my juggling rocks as my humble gift."

"Thank you, Sad Sid," said Princess Minnie. She opened the sack. Inside she found very sparkly rocks indeed! White diamonds, red rubies, and deep-green emeralds! "Oh, my!" exclaimed Princess Minnie. "These sparkly rocks are priceless gems!"

Sir Mickey got an idea. "Listen, Princess. What if we use these jewels to build a water ride? We could use the geyser and the palace moat. Surely people from all over would visit your princess-dom and pay to ride your wild wagon water ride!"

Princess Minnie agreed. "With gems like these, we could build the biggest wild wagon water ride ever! And Sad Sid could run it for us." She turned to the troll. "Sad Sid, would you like to run it?"

"Why, sure I would!" said Sad Sid. And so it came to pass that Princess Minnie built the most spectacular wild wagon water ride the world had ever seen. Sad Sid, the lonely giant troll, ran the ride and officially changed his name to Smiling Sid, the giant no-longer-lonely troll. People came from far and wide to ride the "Wild Wagon Water Ride" and to visit Smiling Sid. Now Princess Minnie can always pay the butcher, the baker, the candlestick maker, the tinker, the tailor, and her knights, Sir Goofy and Sir Mickey (her most favorite knight of all).

Sasha Cohen skates at the 2006 Winter Olympic Games in Turin, Italy. She won the silver medal.

Beauty On Ice

Everyone loves to watch figure skating. The graceful skaters glide, twirl, leap, and spin. The best skaters make it look easy. They are truly amazing. In 2006, three young female U.S. skaters delighted fans with their performances on the ice!

Talented Sasha Cohen, 21, is known for her spins and spirals. She took home three medals in 2006. She skated to the gold at the U.S. Championships—with seven triple jumps. She won the silver medal at the Winter Olympic Games. And she won bronze at the World Championships.

Kimmie Meissner, 16, had a great year, too. She won the silver medal at the U.S. Championships. Then she surprised just about everyone by winning the gold medal at the World Championships. She landed seven triple jumps there. And she loves to do triple-triples—two triple jumps in a row!

Kimmie's rise in figure skating was quick. She won her first gold medal when she was just 13.

Teenager Kimmie Meissner spins her way to the gold medal at the 2006 World Figure Skating Championships.

Starting Young

How do you get to be a champion ice skater? Start young! Like these young skaters, lots of kids learn to skate on local ponds. Kimmie Meissner started when she was 6 years old. Of course, it takes lots and lots of practice to become a champion. And first you have to learn to keep your balance!

Ice Skating Through the Ages

No one knows just when or where ice skating first began. But people have been skating for thousands of years. Long ago, people figured out that the fastest way to cross frozen lakes in winter was to skate across them. Soon they found that skating was also lots of fun!

Skating became even more fun as people learned to make better skates. The first skates had blades made from animal bones. These blades weren't very strong. Then people in northern Europe began to make skates with metal blades. The metal blades were strong and sharp. Now people could skate faster.

Ice skating was hugely popular in the United States in the 1800's. Back then, crowds of skaters glided around frozen ponds on winter days. Some people began to add dance steps to their skating. And that's how figure skating began. Before long, figure skating joined speed skating as a competitive sport.

Another skater who was making her mark in the skating world was 17-year-old Emily Hughes. She's fast on the ice and performs strong spins.

Emily's older sister, Sarah Hughes, won the gold medal at the 2002 Winter Olympic Games. In 2006 it was Emily's turn to be in the Winter Olympics.

Emily joined the U.S. Olympic team at the last minute. One of the team's top skaters, Michelle Kwan, was hurt. Emily took her place. She finished seventh in the competition, right behind Kimmie Meissner.

These young skaters have worked very hard to be as good as they are. They are truly stars on ice!

Above: Skating sisters Sarah (left) and Emily Hughes. Left: Emily on the ice.

This isn't as easy as it looks!

95

The Last Laugh!

What's an ape's favorite junk food?

Potato chimps!

What did one melting icicle say to the other icicle?

Hang in there!

What do you get when you cross a turtle with a porcupine?

A slow-poke!

Why can't you play hide-and-seek with a mountain?

Because it always peaks!

What has two humps and is found at the North Pole?

A lost camel!

What's orange and sounds like a parrot?

A carrot!

Why do skunks like Valentine's Day?

Because they are so scent-imental!